Broken Chains
FREEDOM FROM UNWANTED HABITS AND ADDICTIONS

F. Michael Grubbs, DCoun

ISBN-13: 978-1-7322017-1-2

DEDICATION

This book is dedicated to my good friend, Brian Murray.

FOREWARD

I do not usually write forwards or endorsements for books. Unless I know the man, his ministry and have both read and been impressed with his book, I don't even consider writing one. In this case, I am honored to write this forward. In fact, if Mike had not asked me to write it, I was planning to ask him if I could do so.

I know this man. He is my close friend. I have many friends, but few that are close. The reality is that those who are close will tell you being my friend is not always easy to do. Mike loves me just like I am – warts and all. He is also my life coach. Nobody needs a pastor and a coach like those who pastor and coach thousands. That is especially true for me. Mike has kept the old Ford truck that is my life, out of the ditch and running down the road for the past eight years. No small feat.

I know this book. When Mike put the first draft of this book in my hands months ago, I knew he was on to something. Quite honestly, the book is better than Mike is! God Himself must have helped author the words and truths that follow on these pages. At last – a practical yet correctly theologically based pathway to freedom from addictions. We have needed this book for so long!

I know this need. In my opinion, we are all addicts. We all need help. We all need a Deliverer. From my need to be needed to my friends who are addicted to sex or drugs or alcohol, we are all addicts in desperate need of a Savior and the freedom He can and wants to bring. Addiction to sin is the great equalizer that makes the ground at the foot of the cross level. We are all sinners in need of Jesus.

I know this path. I have struggled with my own addictions for decades. Mike and the truths he shares in this book have been used by Jesus to set me free! And if I can get free – anyone can get free.

This book is not just another way to say the same things over again, those that have been written and said about addiction for the past fifty years. This book is a fresh and practical approach to learning to live free from the chains that so quickly and easily bind us.

Jesus said, "You will know the truth, and the truth will set you free." I pray you will find His truth and His freedom as I have in the truths of this book.

Blessings

Dan Southerland
Church Planter / Pastor / The Movement Group / Kansas City, Kansas
Author / Transitions: Leading Your Church Through Change and Chairtime
Chief Sinner and Lover of Jesus

TABLE OF CONTENTS

BIBLICAL REFERENCE LIST

All Scripture NIV unless otherwise indicated.

NIV   *The Holy Bible, New International Version.* (Grand Rapids: Zondervan Publishing House, 1984).

Other versions are so noted with each reference used.

ESV   *The Holy Bible: English Standard Version* (Wheaton: Standard Bible Society, 2016).

NASB   *New American Standard Bible*: 1995 update. 1995. LaHabra, CA: The Lockman Foundation.

NLT   Tyndale House Publishers, *Holy Bible: New Living Translation* (Carol Stream, IL: Tyndale House Publishers, 2013)

TNIV   *The Holy Bible: Today's New International Version.* (Grand Rapids, MI: Zondervan, 2005).

INTRODUCTION

I have undertaken this project for several reasons. Having read extensively on the subject I found there was a need for a Scriptural basis for addictiveness, liberation, and living free. If the Word of God is clear about what enslaves fallen mankind, what would set him free and how to live in that freedom, we should by all means investigate, understand, and utilize this wisdom.

Having counseled individuals, spouses, and families largely struggling with these realities for more than thirty-five years I have been observing what is classically taught and thought about these habitual and addictive behaviors and the attending spiritual struggle with fear and guilt. I find them to have some success with changing behaviors, that is, patterns of specific behavior. I also find the, now traditional, treatments to have little effect on the heart. To quote Rich Mullins, "The heart of the matter, is a matter of the heart." If the depths of an individual are not substantially changed, but only the outward behavior, then the habit or addiction will transfer to another behavior that the individual will begin to rely on for fulfillment, always false and empty, unless it is God himself. It cannot be a "higher power," whatever that means. This would represent only another strategy to fill the emptiness that cannot be filled (read the book to find out what actually fills that which cannot be filled). A "higher power" is not the highest power it only implies that which is higher than you. Why settle for that which only poses to be absolute when you can have to the fullest him who is sovereign over "all things," him who is ABSOLUTE!

The writing of this book is also a catharsis. I have been the participant in unwanted habits and an addiction in my life. I know firsthand the fear and guilt of being "a helpless, bad individual" and what that does to a person. I also, know firsthand what it is to be freed from the burden, and have lived free for some many years. Can someone say, "Praise the Lord?"

Finally, I have written in this way because I believe that all behavior, especially habits and addictions, but also distractions, defenses, diffusions, secrets, hidings, etc. either will ultimately lead you toward God or away from him. For instance, if I used to use alcohol to numb myself from relationships and their attendant pain and frustration; now I have stopped drinking but when I come home I shut myself off from my wife/husband and children by watching one television show after another, I have accomplished an outward change, but nothing inward or even real. In effect, I have traded one wrong strategy to fill my emptiness with a more acceptable and slightly less destructive behavior (compare the struggle of a child of an alcoholic to a present but non-interactive parent, other than possible physical abuse you will find the damage to be very similar).

I believe that when taught, understood, and applied the truths in this book are effective for freedom and the abundant life that Jesus came to give us. I have seen it work over and over again; rather I should say I have seen HIM work over and over again.

Galatians 5:1 *It is for freedom that Christ has set us free. Stand firm, then, and do not let yourselves be burdened again by a yoke of slavery.*

Let us continue with an understanding of "addictiveness."

PART 1 ADDICTIVENESS

F. Michael Grubbs

CHAPTER 1
ADDICTION'S DEFINITION

The definition of addiction is manifold, but the key word is inability, the inability of an individual to cease or have power over a behavior or behaviors. The individual is unable to manage or control the area of weakness and struggle. The classic understanding of addiction is behavioristic. The beginning and ending of therapy for addiction is behavior. Certainly, God cares greatly about our behavior; a great portion of both the Old Testament and the New Testament is dedicated to speaking about the behavior of God's people. Spiritually, behavior can be broken down into two categories. The first is God-pleasing behavior. The second is man-pleasing (self-pleasing) behavior.

A good biblical example of this is found a few years after the Garden of Eden was removed from mankind. It reads like this:

> **Genesis 4:2-8** *Now Abel kept flocks, and Cain worked the soil. [3] In the course of time Cain brought some of the fruits of the soil as an offering to the LORD. [4] But Abel brought fat portions from some of the firstborn of his flock. The LORD looked with favor on Abel and his offering, [5] but on Cain and his offering he did not look with favor. So Cain was very angry, and his face was downcast. [6] Then the LORD said to Cain, "Why are you angry? Why is your face downcast? [7] If you do what is right, will you not*

*be accepted? But if you do not do what is right, sin is crouching
at your door; it desires to have you, but you must master it."* [8]
*Now Cain said to his brother Abel, "Let's go out to the field."
And while they were in the field, Cain attacked his brother Abel
and killed him.*

God speaking to Cain in verse six states the dilemma. If Cain
would be a God-pleaser, he would put away his anger and seek to
please God, not himself. God, early in his Word then states a
principle of the fallen world which is true for all of mankind, *"sin
is crouching at your door; it desires to have you, but you must
master it."* This is the same door of the heart at which Jesus stands
and knocks in Revelation 3:20 (NLT) *"Look! I stand at the door
and knock. If you hear my voice and open the door, I will come in,
and we will share a meal together as friends.* The man-pleasing
(self-pleasing) part of Cain won out in this instance and God's
judgment was harsh and quick.

In the New Testament a similar thought is found:

> **Romans 8:5-9** *Those who live according to the <u>sinful nature
> have their minds set on what that nature</u> desires; but those who
> live in accordance with the Spirit have their minds set on what
> the Spirit desires.* [6] *The mind of sinful man is death, but the mind
> controlled by the Spirit is life and peace;* [7] *the sinful mind is
> hostile to God. It does not submit to God's law, nor can it do so.*
> [8] <u>*Those controlled by the sinful nature cannot please God.*</u> [9] *You,
> however, are controlled not by the sinful nature but by the Spirit,
> if the Spirit of God lives in you.* (Underlining is the author's)

Here we see that the mind set on the desires of the sinful nature
(man/self-pleasing) is hostile to God and cannot please God. The
mind set on the Spirit (God) however, brings life and peace. The
question is which is the controlling factor? The Spirit led life is
God-pleasing and the sinful nature is a life that is man-pleasing
(self-pleasing). These are declared to be in conflict with each
other. The behaviors of each will be drastically different and
mutually opposed. All addictions wholly arise out of the sinful

nature and are designed to please the self.

A person suffering addiction may learn to stop the addictive behavior, but does that mean that he/she is a God-pleaser? Does that mean that he/she is living life abundantly? Does that mean that he/she is free to love that life that God has called him/her to live?

God, through the prophet Jeremiah spoke to Israel; God was going to send Israel into captivity because of their evil behavior, because of their betrayal of himself. They would be in captivity for seventy years. At the end of that time God promised freedom for them for he had called them to a life that he had planned for them.

> **Jeremiah 29:11-14** *For I know the plans I have for you," declares the Lord, "plans to prosper you and not to harm you, plans to give you hope and a future. [12] Then you will call upon me and come and pray to me, and I will listen to you. [13] You will seek me and find me when you seek me with all your heart. [14] I will be found by you," declares the Lord, "and will bring you back from captivity."*

God says that when we seek him with ALL our heart we will find him and he will set us free, bringing us back from captivity. The mind, will, and emotions (soul) must be centered on him, wholly, seeking him with all of our heart! Then we can experience his prosperous plan with hope for the future of freedom he has planned for us. Those of us who have been caught in addiction have a promise from God. First, we must understand our own nature and the mechanism of addiction.

HONEST QUESTIONS LEADING TO FREEDOM

1. Are you a man (self) pleaser or a God pleaser?

   Both

2. Which do you want to be?

   God pleaser

Both Jesus and sin are knocking at the door of our heart. It is our choice to choose who to let in.

God pleasing = peace and life.

Sin is destructive and painful to our own body.

F. Michael Grubbs

CHAPTER 2
CORE ISSUES

In order to discover the core issues we face as humans we must return to the beginning. How did God create us and how were we to find life (not existence, but Life)?

The first time in all of God's creative work where he saw something "not good" is found in **Genesis 2:18** *The LORD God said, "It is not good for the man to be alone. I will make a helper suitable for him."* God, in his creation, had declared all else to be good. Man was to be "in relationship," first, with God and with Eve, Adam's counterpart. After God "made" Eve from Adam's rib Adam woke and beheld his mate. **Genesis 2:25** *The man and his wife were both naked, and they felt no shame.* Nakedness without shame, in this text implies that there was nothing hidden. No history to hide, nothing of self to protect, no secret thoughts, no hidden motives, no buried pain, no pride, nothing unforgiven, in fact all was open and pure between the man and the woman and their God. As God dwells in relationship, within himself, Father, Son, and Spirit (the mystery of the Trinity), God intended for man to dwell in relationship with him and with each other. **Relationship is a key element in God's plan for mankind**.

God had planted a garden he called Eden. In this garden he placed all manner of trees, both for beauty and for food, one for life and one for knowledge (the forbidden tree). God gave man purpose: **Genesis 1:26** God *blessed them and said to them, "Be fruitful and increase in number; fill the earth and subdue it. Rule over the fish of the sea and the birds of the air and over every living creature that moves on the ground."* **Genesis 2:15** The LORD *God took the man and put him in the Garden of Eden to work it and take care of it.* God's purpose was for man to enjoy the work that he gave him to do. This work was beyond man, he was certainly not prepared to "rule" over all the creatures of the earth and to tend this magnificent garden (he probably figured out how to 'be fruitful and increase in number'). Yet there is no indication that man was anxious about fulfilling his purpose. This is perhaps because he was in relationship with the God of the purpose. **Purpose, significance, function are key elements in God's plan for mankind**.

To summarize, man's soul was filled with relationship and purpose. This gave him a life of meaning, a life of infinite interest and work, the life that God desired for his favored of all creation.

HONEST QUESTIONS LEADING TO FREEDOM

1. What would it be like to be naked (totally exposed inside and out, nothing hidden, nothing secret)?

   Transparent, not filled with shame or unclean.

2. With what two things did God fill man's soul?

   relationship and purpose. We have that ability to have both with God.

Notes and Thoughts:

We have a spring to go to. The
living water. Let it fill our soul
with relationship and purpose.

CHAPTER 3
WRONG STRATEGIES

Jeremiah 2:13 "My people have committed two sins: They have forsaken me, the spring of living water, and have dug their own cisterns, broken cisterns that cannot hold water."

One day the Lord took the man and put him in the garden and gave him one rule.

Genesis 2:15-17 The Lord God took the man and put him in the Garden of Eden to work it and take care of it. [16] And the Lord God commanded the man, "You are free to eat from any tree in the garden; [17] but you must not eat from the tree of the knowledge of good and evil, for when you eat of it you will surely die."

This one rule was not prohibitive but was protective. The garden as well as the creation was so marvelous and every provision was made for the living of each and every creature that the "one rule" should not have been a temptation for Adam and Eve. Eve was then made from man and they lived in the garden of God.

Genesis 3:1-6 Now the serpent was more crafty than any of the wild animals the Lord God had made. He said to the woman, "Did God really say, 'You must not eat from any tree in the garden'?" [2] The woman said to the serpent, "We may eat fruit from the trees in the garden, [3] but God did say, 'you must not eat fruit from the tree that is in the middle of the garden, and you must not touch it, or you will die.' " [4] "You will not surely die," the serpent said to the woman. [5] "For God knows that when you eat of it your eyes will be opened, and you will be like God, knowing good and evil." [6] When the woman saw that the fruit of the tree was good for food and pleasing to the eye, and also desirable for gaining wisdom, she took some and ate it. She also gave some to her husband, who was with her, and he ate it.

The crafty serpent, whose desire was to wreak havoc on God's creation, one day had a conversation with Eve (Adam was standing beside her, perhaps in a catatonic state). He begins by asking a seemingly innocent question and Eve answers the question as honestly as she was able. If you compare the "one rule" that God gave to Adam before Eve was made with how she answered the serpent (cp. **Genesis 2:15** with **Genesis 3:2**) you will find that these words are added to God's "one rule." The words are: "and you must not touch it." (It is my belief that Adam added these words to "make sure" that Eve did not go near the Tree of the knowledge of good and evil; it may have been his undoing.) The crafty serpent challenges her by saying that "you will not surely die." Check it out in several translations; the meaning is the same. It is not certain that you will die. The enemy of our souls will deal in half-truths in order to make us stumble; it is one of his favorite tricks. He added a twist, accusing God of keeping something from them, something to make them subject to God, something to keep them ignorant. It is the same human attitude that makes us want to be a teen when we are eleven years old, then an adult when we are sixteen, and to experience things we are not mature enough to experience always wanting what is not good for us at the time. In this case he accused God of keeping them from wisdom, from knowing good from evil. Oh, that we only knew good and not evil!

Eve accepted the challenge and we are exposed to her thoughts. This is most significant! First, she perceived that the tree was good for food (like every other fruit-bearing tree that God had provided). Second, she saw that the fruit of the tree was beautiful (like the entire garden). Third, she saw that if she ate of the fruit she would gain wisdom! What happened next is most crucial in my opinion. She took some! (Took it in her hand, "touched" it). It is my contention that she touched it as a test and she found God to be untrue, for as she touched it she did not die (her body did not cease to function, her mind did not stop thinking). The added words, 'and you must not touch it' proved to be incentive to mistrust the "one rule" (and the God who made the rule) **then she ate it** (actually breaking the one rule). Then she gave it to her husband who was with her and he ate of it. Ever after it is man's chief difficulty, to trust God in what he says!

> **Genesis 3:7-8** *Then the eyes of both of them were opened, and they realized they were naked; so they sewed fig leaves together and made coverings for themselves. [8] Then the man and his wife heard the sound of the LORD God as he was walking in the garden in the cool of the day, and they hid from the LORD God among the trees of the garden.*

Adam woke up! He became conscious of what had happened. They realized they were naked (meaning that now they had much to hide, secret motivations they did not wish to come to light). They did what they could to cover their nakedness, but the relationship between them was broken. They heard God in the garden and they hid themselves from him. Their relationship with God was broken. In both their souls was opened a **bottomless pit** of relationship; the shattered relationship between them and God and between each other.

> **Genesis 3:9-13** *But the LORD God called to the man, "Where are you?" [10] He answered, "I heard you in the garden, and I was afraid because I was naked; so I hid."*
> *[11] And he said, "Who told you that you were naked? Have you eaten from the tree that I commanded you not to eat from?" [12] The man said, "The woman you put here with me—she gave me some fruit from the tree, and I ate it." [13] Then the LORD God said to the woman, "What is this you have done?" The woman said, "The serpent deceived me, and I ate."*

blaming each other

Hiding from God, then blaming the woman (and second-handedly God, because he had given her to him), the woman blaming the serpent (that she and Adam should have had dominion over) but never confessing the true motivations of each (they were now hiding truth, secretive), God pronounces the punishment and then removes them from the garden of God. Shame is a powerful motivator for the struggling person. Blame and lies, hiding and keeping secret that of which we are ashamed becomes a second and companion nature to the addictive person. — *hiding.*

> **Genesis 3:20-24** *Adam named his wife Eve, because she would become the mother of all the living. ²¹ The LORD God made garments of skin for Adam and his wife and clothed them. ²² And the LORD God said, "The man has now become like one of us, knowing good and evil. He must not be allowed to reach out his hand and take also from the tree of life and eat, and live forever." ²³ So the LORD God banished him from the Garden of Eden to work the ground from which he had been taken. ²⁴ After he drove the man out, he placed on the east side of the Garden of Eden cherubim and a flaming sword flashing back and forth to guard the way to the tree of life.*

God then took Adam and Eve and removed the garden from them. This kept them from eating of the tree of life in the fallen state in which they now found themselves. **Verse 24** is particularly curious. All translations will account that the way **TO** the tree of life is guarded, kept, preserved. I believe that this is a reference to the way out of the bondage to sin (emptiness of relationship and purpose) and into the freedom of God's intended way of life for mankind. It is significant that at the very eviction from the tree of life God preserves the way to it.

The end result of the fall of man is that there are now two bottomless pits in the soul. **The first of these bottomless pits is for relationship.** Throughout history we have demonstrated over and over again that we will do anything and everything to fill this bottomless pit in our souls. From adultery to war and everything in between we have been trying to fill this open-ended pit in unending efforts. All manner of sin and human invention has been expended to fill this bottomless pit, yet it remains bottomless, ultimately empty. This emptiness is one source of addiction; the feelings of abandonment, not fitting in, being misunderstood, etc.

Relationship has to do with connection. The way in which two or more people relate or connect with one another is a determining factor in identity. We identify ourselves in terms of how others love us, relate to us, and connect with us. This is why we form teams, groups, clubs, societies, associations, leagues, fellowships, fraternities, sororities, etc. We identify with people like ourselves who are committed to similar ideals, philosophies, causes, and activities but also committed to each other on many different levels. WE WANT TO BELONG! We also WANT TO BE WANTED! This bottomless pit in the soul can be illustrated by couples who have been faithfully married for forty years. They nevertheless, each need to be told and shown that they are loved by their spouse. This is true regardless of gender. Why? It is because the pit is BOTTOMLESS. We cannot fill it. This bottomless pit craves to be filled and we will try to fill it using any and every means we think will work. **Addictions and habits are traps that ensnare us into thinking that a substance or activity will fill the pit.** Worse, it seems to fill it, for a while. But a bottomless pit is bottomless. The human soul insatiably craves love. It is always asking, "Am I loveable?" Sound hopeless? Keep reading.

The second of these bottomless pits is purpose, significance, or impact. Since God's original purpose for man to govern the world, all its creatures, and to tend God's own garden was withdrawn; man has sought to fill the bottomless pit of purpose with something, anything as significant as the original purpose. Nothing we have attempted to do has even come close to the magnitude of that first purpose. To rule the people of the earth, to build a tower to reach the heavens, to conquer space and to discover the laws of science, all this and many other endeavors both large and small can never fill this bottomless pit in our soul since abandoning God's first purpose. This emptiness is the second source of addiction. The feelings of unworthiness, not measuring up, having no direction, or, ambition to accomplish, climbing up and over to get to the top and finding the top just as empty and many other scenarios.

17

The result of these two bottomless pits in man's soul is that we employ all manner of wrong strategies in a relentless effort to do the impossible, to satisfy the insatiable emptiness of the soul apart from the God who made it.

> ***Jeremiah 2:13*** *"My people have committed two sins: They have forsaken me, the spring of living water, and have dug their own cisterns, broken cisterns that cannot hold water.".*

God is the spring of living water. I picture this as an artesian well, coming from deep in the earth and finding its way to the surface by way of pressure; it is cool, pure, clean and vital. By forsaking God we do not drink and bathe in this life-giving water, we choose something very different. The first sin we, everyone born of Adam, commit is forsaking God. One of the most comprehensive definitions of sin in the Bible is found in **Isaiah 53:6**, the first part; *We all, like sheep, have gone astray, each of us has turned to his own way;* When we go our own way, we are straying from the path that God has set for us. We are forsaking the spring of living water. Jesus said that the path for his people was narrow and straight. **Matthew 7:14** *But small is the gate and narrow the road that leads to life, and only a few find it.*

The second sin is digging our own cisterns, broken cisterns, that is trying to sustain our lives by our own doing. These cisterns were filled by catching rainwater in an effort to preserve the water for use when the rains ceased in the drier times of the year. In more modern thought, I picture the cistern like a concrete birdbath in the back yard. In the summer when the weather is hot and little rain falls, the birdbath might be filled occasionally or only by sprinklers employed for watering the grass or garden. Birds are notorious for not being house-broken. In other words, they are not inhibited from "using the rest room" in the birdbath. Further, they are washing themselves there, flipping the water on their feathers to wash off the dust and pollen, etc. And furthermore, there grows in the bottom of the summer birdbath a green algae substance that cannot be healthy. Think of this, rather than seeking the free-flowing fountain of crystal clear, clean, pure, cool water from which to drink, we turn to the summer birdbath in the back yard from which to quench our thirst! Unthinkable? Reread the statement from **Jeremiah in 2:13**!

How does this apply to our core issues of RELATIONSHIP and PURPOSE? Remember these core issues are "bottomless pits" within our souls. They demand to be filled. They create an insatiable thirst that calls our attention constantly. Try working out, or working outside in the heat, sweating without drinking anything for a couple of hours. Soon, all you can think about is drinking! The body is conspiring with the mind to re-hydrate itself. The longer you postpone the re-hydration the more the body calls for water. Soon you begin to slow down, the tongue swells and the throat closes, and dizziness sets in. This is all in effort to get you to pay attention to this great thirst and satisfy it.

Likewise, the bottomless pits constantly call attention to themselves. Our souls demand to be filled with relationship and purpose. Having forsaken the spring of living water, we return again and again to the birdbath filling ourselves with what is putrid, rank, and rotting. These are "wrong strategies" to fill these pits without bottom in our souls. We may use alcohol, drugs (of all kinds), sex, gambling, eating, entertainment, work, hobbies, success, etc. in an effort to fill these pits, but they have no bottom. We may feel "full" for a few minutes or anesthetized for a while and temporarily feel fulfilled, but the thirst returns and returns and returns again. This is the beginning of addiction. No matter how much you gamble, no matter how much pornography you view, no matter how much alcohol you consume, no matter how many sexual acts with however many partners, no matter what kind or how much dope you take or smoke, no matter how much work you do or how many promotions you receive, no matter how much stuff you accumulate, no matter how much you eat or how many movies you watch you are always yet and again EMPTY! There is no end to the "wrong strategies" we employ to try to fill these bottomless pits, yet they remain bottomless. (Many of these things are not, in themselves evil but they are wrong strategies for fulfillment.)

The human nature, that has forsaken God, is creative and innovative in its endeavor to fill these bottomless pits.

> **Ephesians 2:1-3** *As for you, you were dead in your transgressions and sins, [2] in which you used to live when you*

followed the ways of this world and of the ruler of the kingdom of the air, the spirit who is now at work in those who are disobedient. ³ All of us also lived among them at one time, gratifying the cravings of our sinful nature and following its desires and thoughts. Like the rest, we were by nature objects of wrath.

Using our language, being dead in transgressions and sins is our continual drinking from the birdbath, wrong strategies for filling our bottomless pits. The ruler of the kingdom of the air is Satan, that same one, who lured Adam and Eve to satisfy their desire to be wise, like God. This one is at work in all who are disobedient, all those who have forsaken God, the spring of living water. The next sentence is the eye-opener. This sinful nature craves! Webster defines "crave" in this way:

1 synonyms BEG, appeal, beseech, brace, entreat, implore, importune, plead, pray, supplicate
2 synonyms DESIRE, choose, covet, desiderate, want, wish
3 synonyms LONG, ache, dream, hanker, hunger, lust, pine, sigh, suspire, and thirst
4 synonyms DEMAND, ask, call (for), necessitate, require, take[1]

The insatiable thirst of the bottomless pits in our souls creates this craving. The gratification of this craving is what we seek with every fiber of our beings, an attempt to fill the emptiness that drives us. Next, we see that the sinful nature is not simply driven by insatiability but it also desires and wants; it believes it is entitled to be fulfilled! These desires are tailored to our personality, I like ketchup on my burger, you like mayonnaise. Personal likes, that which is desirable to us, the things, which we prefer, favor. It, the sinful nature, also thinks! One way of understanding this "thinking" might be "scheming." The idea that our minds are put to finding ways to satisfy this thirst, this craving, and this insatiability. This concept of scheming or thinking includes strategizing, regarding the filling of the un-fillable pits in our souls. Everyone has experienced this. We decide we want (desire) some ice cream and we know we shouldn't have any.

Next our minds begin to justify and rationalize the having and enjoying of the ice cream. Then we begin to figure out how we can get our spouse to get the ice cream so we don't have to get up to get it, or we might think, "I will wait until they go to bed and get the ice cream so I do not have to listen to the reasons why I should not have the ice cream before I go to bed." This is a greatly simplified and naïve example. Our sinful nature is operating wrong strategies in complex and multifarious ways in a continual effort to fill the bottomless pits in our souls.

It is the craving that drives us, motivates us, and compels us to get satisfaction (Read the lyrics to the 1965 Hit Song "I can't get no satisfaction" by the Rolling Stones). It is the desire, which directs and selects the object of satisfaction. It is the thinking, scheming that devises the way to obtain the satisfaction. **This is the essence of addictiveness**.

I choose Jesus.

HONEST QUESTIONS LEADING TO FREEDOM

1. "Blame and lies, hiding and keeping secret that of which we are ashamed becomes a second and companion nature to the addictive person."

    a.   Is this true of you? In what ways?

    I hide my lustful desires and masturbation.

    b.   To whom do you fully disclose?

    My sister but she doesn't fully hold me accountable.

    c.   Who could you trust to be fully disclosed?

    I dont Know. Kelly? Courtney? Abby?

2. What "wrong strategies" are you employing to fill your "bottomless pits?"

    Lies, deceit that it is not wrong.

    I dont want this to leak into my relationships and spoil a good thing. Or to take captive my soul and my holiness.

Notes and Thoughts:

F. Michael Grubbs

CHAPTER 4
HABITS AND HABITUATION

All individuals, families, groups of individuals form habits in their behaviors. Try this next time you shower; if you typically begin at a certain place on your body, begin in an opposite place. You will find this extremely frustrating and will soon be completely lost as to how to complete the process. The last time I tried this I became so perturbed that I had to begin again and had to start over the way I always do, what a relief! Habits in and of themselves are not critical. Sometimes, however where sinful action is involved, habits can be very distressing. They will invariably arise from one or more wrong strategies to fill one or both bottomless pits in the soul. For instance, I may be feeling upset with my boss at work for a poor performance evaluation, which I do not think I deserve, the abyss in my soul for significance begins to act up, I need to feel good about myself. My "go to" action is chocolate (substitute your preference here) so I go to the cupboard and eat half of a pound of Cadbury. This makes me feel better so the next time and the next time again I turn to chocolate for gratification. This seems innocent enough. Years later, however, when the arteries are clogged with cholesterol and you are 40 pounds overweight you might think differently.

Webster defines habit as: **¹hab•it** ha-bət *noun*

1: the prevailing disposition or character of a person's thoughts and feelings : mental makeup

2: a settled tendency or usual manner of behavior (her *habit* of taking a morning walk)

   3   **a:** a behavior pattern acquired by frequent repetition or physiologic exposure that shows itself in regularity or increased facility of performance

      b: an acquired mode of behavior that has become nearly or completely involuntary (got

      up early from force of *habit)*[1]

The definition begins as thoughts and feelings, progresses to customary behavior, becomes a pattern (created by repetition), and finally the habit becomes 'nearly or completely involuntary.' This progression, when attached with addictive behaviors, will lead to habituation. A definition of habituation: "The result of repeated consumption of a drug, which produces a psychological, but no physical dependence. The psychological dependence produces a desire (not a compulsion) to continue taking drugs or alcohol for a sense of improved well-being.) Habituated persons go deeper and deeper into the habit in order to get the same gratification as when the habit began. When the individual discovers an inability to control or cease the behavior the classification then becomes addiction." (definition taken from Candeocan.com). Many sinful activities can follow this same pathway and entrap even believing people. In an article on the Candeocan.com website Dr. Hyde responds to a question asked by a reader.

> "My Response: I have found that generally, consistent porn users increase both the time on the computer, and also become more deviant. This is due to the brain's natural tendency to habituate to an activity and build up a tolerance, thus requiring greater levels of stimulation to get the same high. This is the case with any addiction. Tolerance with alcohol builds up so that more and more alcohol needs to be consumed in order to get drunk or get the "buzz". It's the same with Porn.[2]

The apostle Paul, writer of many New Testament books says,

Romans 7:18-25 "*[18] I know that nothing good lives in me, that is, in my sinful nature. For I have the desire to do what is good, but I cannot carry it out. [19] For what I do is not the good I want to do; no, the evil I do not want to do—this I keep on doing. [20] Now if I do what I do not want to do, it is no longer I who do it, but it is sin living in me that does it. [21] So I find this law at work: When I want to do good, evil is right there with me. [22] For in my inner being I delight in God's law; [23] but I see another law at work in the members of my body, waging war against the law of my mind and making me a prisoner of the law of sin at work within my members. [24] What a wretched man I am! Who will rescue me from this body of death? [25] Thanks be to God— through Jesus Christ our Lord! So then, I myself in my mind am a slave to God's law, but in the sinful nature a slave to the law of sin.*

Paul states clearly that there is a war going on in the individual (himself), his behavior is "the evil I do not want to do": THIS HE KEEPS DOING! When he wants to do good (all addictive people want to do good), evil is alongside him (remember Cain in chapter 1 of this book *[7] If you do what is right, will you not be accepted? But if you do not do what is right, <u>sin is crouching at your door; it desires to have you, but you must master it)</u>* **Genesis 4:7**. The war is fought in the mind! (Verse 23 above) We have all had thoughts something like this; "I have had a hard day, I deserve to have a couple drinks to relax." "My spouse has been really difficult, I deserve..." "The pressure I am under is really intense, I need to..." These thoughts and many more come easily to the *mind set on what the sinful nature desires.* (**Romans 8:5**) There is no shortage of rationalizations and justifications for our habits or addictive behaviors.

HONEST QUESTIONS LEADING TO FREEDOM

1. Where are you stuck? What habits can you not give up?

2. What "wrong strategies" do you employ to keep your habits and addictions?

3. How are you justifying and/or rationalizing your habits and addictions?

Notes and Thoughts:

F. Michael Grubbs

CHAPTER 5
DEPENDENCIES

Dependency is the result of being trapped in a wrong strategy to fill the bottomless pits in our souls. The wrong strategies can be anything that we have used to *"gratify the cravings of our sinful nature."* (**Ephesians 2:3**) Typically they might include; alcohol, marijuana, gambling, prescription and illegal drugs, pornography, sex, eating (or not eating), overworking, procrastinating, etc. etc. Some dependencies that may or may not be addictions include; video games, television, movies, work (employment or just constantly working at something), spending money, shoplifting, driving fast, using the internet (Facebook, Twitter, etc.), risky behaviors, etc. If you <u>depend</u> on it for peace, safety, gratification, satisfaction, sense of well-being or flight from difficulty, it is or will become a point of addictiveness. **Colossians 2:8** *See to it that no one takes you captive through hollow and deceptive philosophy, which depends on human tradition and the basic principles of this world rather than on Christ.* Paul is here warning the Colossian people about possible captivity. Who can **first** take you captive? The answer is you! Hollow and deceptive philosophy can be the idea that you actually can fill up your emptiness if you just get enough of "it" or the right mix of this and/or that. Human tradition might be what you have seen your parents or relatives or friends do that gives the appearance of being fulfilled (workaholic sons often become like their workaholic fathers, etc.) Basic principles of this (fallen) world might be efforts to satisfy the lust of the eyes (obtaining what you see), the lust of the flesh (physical appetites), and the boastful pride of life (fame and fortune) **1 John 2:16** (NASB). **When you rely on something other than Jesus Christ to fill your emptiness you are opening yourself up to becoming captive.** First, it becomes habit (quick gratification). Next, when it becomes habituated, you need more and more of it. Then, when you rely on it to provide some peace (mellow out), to relieve frustration or anger, to disengage from the difficulties of life, to be a hiding place from yourself and others, to alleviate stress, to take the edge off; **you are imprisoned.** When you get to this stage, where you cannot imagine life without your dependency, then you are trapped, ensnared, made captive, enslaved. As has been said before these dependencies can be any number of things, activities, substances, even people (co-dependency). It all amounts to the same thing. Relying on something other than God to fill our ruthless, relentless need to fill our soul's emptiness through the use of these wrong strategies equals slavery. Jesus said that the sinner is a slave to sin. I believe that in our context this can mean that when we endeavor to fill our emptiness ourselves and have become entrapped in the effort, we then are made captive. **John 8:34** *Jesus replied, "I tell you the truth, everyone who sins is a slave to sin.* The continual use of wrong strategies has devastating consequences. Addiction carries with it a sense of embarrassment, shame, disgrace, guilt, helplessness and hopelessness. Most people, who are dependent on something that is not God, suffer lack of dignity, esteem, respect, value, and worth. They have lost their sense of belonging to anything worthwhile. Addiction further separates us from relationship and purpose, but the addicted person cannot seem to stop trying to fill the bottomless holes in his/her soul. It becomes a vicious cycle of self-loathing and self-medicating. Albert Einstein said, 'the definition of insanity is doing the same thing over and over again expecting a different result.' In this sense addiction is insanity!

HONEST QUESTIONS LEADING TO FREEDOM

1. What habits would you like to be free from?

2. What do you "rely" on when you are stressed?

3. What are your "dependencies?"

4. To what are you addicted?

Notes and Thoughts:

PART 2 LIBERATION

F. Michael Grubbs

CHAPTER 6
LIBERATION

Gal 5:1 *It is for freedom that Christ has set us free. Stand firm, then, and do not let yourselves be burdened again by a yoke of slavery.*

God intends for you to be free! The reason he sent his son to the world is that we may be freed from the bondage to sin. **Romans 8:1-2** *Therefore, there is now no condemnation for those who are in Christ Jesus, ² because through Christ Jesus the law of the Spirit of life set me free from the law of sin and death.* We have failed to keep God's laws, we have tried to fill and fulfill ourselves countless times with many different strategies. We have become dependent on designs of our own making, and we may have become enslaved by these false strategies; believing that just a little more, just one more time will fill the emptiness in our souls.

WHAT FILLS *BOTTOMLESS* PITS?

Most of you are thinking, "What a stupid question, it is bottomless, nothing fills it, ever! If you answered this way you would be wrong!

SOMETHING *INFINITE* FILLS UP BOTTOMLESS PITS!!

Only the infinite, almighty God can fill the bottomless pit for relationship in your soul! Only God can fill the bottomless pit for purpose and significance in your soul! God longs to fill you full to overflowing and only HE can!!!

What is your part in this tremendous promise? Just this; you must **want** to be free! You must **want freedom** more than you want the thing that has you in chains. You must **want** to be free more than you want to fill your cravings and desires. You must be **desperate for freedom**, hating the captivity, longing for liberation. And you must trust that He is **big enough** to fill your emptiness!

Psalms 37:4-6 *Delight yourself in the LORD and he will give you the desires of your heart. ⁵Commit your way to the LORD; trust in him and he will do this: ⁶He will make your righteousness shine like the dawn, the justice of your cause like the noonday sun.* The Psalmist is saying that when God becomes FIRST in your mind and life then what you desire foremost will be given to you. When God is first, only holy things will be desired! The Psalmist goes on to say that a commitment must be made. That God's way is right, that he has your way, your path set out for you to follow and that this way will lead to satisfaction of your soul! He continues, "Trust in him and he will do this." What a great promise! When we give ourselves wholly over to God we will lack nothing! When we give ourselves wholly to God he will free us of our captivity. **Jeremiah 29:13** *You will seek me and find me when you seek me with all your heart. ¹⁴ I will be found by you," declares the LORD, "and will bring you back from captivity.* God is calling you out of darkness into his marvelous light (**1 Peter 2:9 NASB**). The difficult thing is to recognize your hunger and thirst for him and his life, as opposed to gratifying the craving of your sinful nature (**Ephesians 2:3**). Paul came to this conclusion when writing to the Galatians in the second chapter; *²⁰ I have been crucified with Christ and I no longer live, but Christ lives in me. The life I live in the body, I live by faith in the Son of God, who loved me and gave himself for me.* (**Galatians 2:20**) Paul was drawing his life from the infinite One who could fill his bottomless pits to overflowing; **Romans 8:11** *And if the Spirit of him who raised Jesus from the dead is living in you, he who raised Christ from the dead will also give life to your mortal bodies through his Spirit, who lives in you.*

This truth could be demonstrated by Nebuchadnezzar, the king of the Babylonians who desired to fill his bottomless pit for purpose by the wrong strategy of being worshiped. God then shows himself in the furnace with his servants. Nebuchadnezzar observed the miracle but refused to recognize (confess) his reliance on self. God bound him in the chains of his mind for seven years, and then he liberated him! Get your Bible and read Daniel, chapters 3 and 4.

This truth can also be demonstrated by Jeff's fear of failure, a chain that bound him for most of his life. His wrong strategies for purpose and relationship ended in alcoholism and an affair. As God was liberating him, Jeff's answer to his fear of failure was to "never make another mistake." This was another loop in the impossible chain that bound him. As Jesus set him free and became Jeff's one and only source, Jeff began to invite Jesus into every meeting, every conference, every planning time, every conversation. He is drinking from the spring of living water today and is freely worshiping God.

This truth can be demonstrated in Susan whose wrong strategy to fill her bottomless pit for relationship was eating a pound of chocolate after consuming a one-pound bag of chips while watching romance movies. Now she is dining on the "Bread of Life," not merely in the Bible but in true relationship with him! Now that the vertical relationship is all important she has begun many healthy horizontal relationships and the pit in her soul is filled to overflowing.

HONEST QUESTIONS LEADING TO FREEDOM

1. What has you in chains in a never-ending effort to fill your emptiness?

2. Do you want to be free more than you want what has enslaved you?

3. Do you trust God enough to believe he can liberate you and can give you overflowing Life?

Notes and Thoughts:

CHAPTER 7
RECOGNITION AND SUBMISSION

We must recognize that what we have been relying on to fill up our emptiness in relationship and purpose is <u>not working</u>. As long as we insist on filling our own emptiness, no matter what strategy we employ, whatever we try will fail. **Proverbs 21:2** *All a man's ways seem right to him, but the LORD weighs the heart.* Since God is not involved, indeed it cannot produce the fulfillment that we seek. When we recognize that the things we think will satisfy, no matter how many times we try them or to what degree we pursue them, will only leave us still empty and wanting; we are then on the way toward God. When we come to the "end of ourselves," that is, the end of our resources to make lasting satisfaction in relationships, we finally prove God right and ourselves deficient to fill our emptiness. No human can, of themselves, fill their emptiness; only God in his infinite Being can fill our insatiability for belonging, for counting for something. When we come to the "end of ourselves," that is, the end of our resources to make lasting significance of our lives (I count for something, I matter in this world), we finally prove God right and ourselves deficient to fulfill our worth, our importance. No job, promotion, accumulation of possession, accomplishment, achievement, success, deed, feat, or exploit will satisfy the insatiability for significance in your soul. Only God's unique purpose for you can fill you.

Another word for this recognition is confession. We must confess the inability to fill ourselves. When we confess, we are not telling the omniscient (all-knowing) God something he does not know. Rather, we are holding a mirror up to ourselves and "seeing" the truth of who we are and what motivates us. **1 John 1:9** *If we confess our sins, he is faithful and just and will forgive us our sins and purify us from all unrighteousness.* (sins = wrong strategies) When we confess (recognize) how we have been conducting our lives, that is, having taken charge of our lives, attempting to fill the bottomless pits in our soul with our own wisdom, ignoring the God who made us; God shows up and not only forgives us but **purifies us from all unrighteousness.** *Purify* is an ongoing action verb indicating a continuous purification. As we 'keep on' confessing, he 'keeps on' purifying. Confession is a process of looking in the mirror and allowing Jesus to fill us and change us.

Paul says to us in **Titus 2:11-14** *For the grace of God that brings salvation has appeared to all men.* [12] *It (the grace of God) teaches us to say "No" to ungodliness and worldly passions, and to live self-controlled, upright and godly lives in this present age,* [13] *while we wait for the blessed hope—the glorious appearing of our great God and Savior, Jesus Christ,* [14] *who gave himself for us to redeem us from all wickedness and to purify for himself a people that are his very own, eager to do what is good.* It is God's grace that teaches us to say "no." In light of his amazing grace, that is my forgiveness, my favor, my adoption; I have a choice! I can pursue fulfillment on my own which has always and always will fail; or I can pursue fulfillment by surrender to God's grace and say "NO! I will live by God, today! He is purifying me and making me desire what is good to do! What is good to say! What is good to think! I belong to God and he fills me to the fullest!

Recognition or confession leads to **submission**. I must see now that "my way" has done nothing but lead to frustration and emptiness. **Proverbs 14:12** *There is a way that seems right to a man, but in the end it leads to death.* The things I have heavily invested in to make my life complete are a charade, a sham, a fraud that has left me <u>without purpose</u>, left me <u>without love</u>. "Now God, I need you to take over my life. According to your greatness and your promises fill me to overflowing with a relationship of perfect love and your good purpose."

Galatians 5:1 *It is for freedom that Christ has set us free. Stand firm, then, and do not let yourselves be burdened again by a yoke of slavery.*

Jesus, in obedience to the Father, came to set us free! We need to stand on his promise, to trust that he is able to fulfill it. When we stand firm on him who is the "rock," we are trusting that the God of the universe, who made all that we can see, hear, taste, touch and smell is good, always good, and never less than good. AND HE LOVES ME! Why then, would we return to slavery? Why then, would we be like the animals; **2 Peter 2:22** *Of them the proverbs are true: "A dog returns to its vomit," and, "A sow that is washed goes back to her wallowing in the mud."*?

The beginning of being free from ourselves and our sinful strategies is to recognize and reject the sinful strategies to fill our emptiness (bird bath water) and drink deeply and often of the "Spring of Living water." In this way we are fulfilled, even to overflowing, which not only is a blessing to us but to others.

How do we then proceed on the path toward liberation? Let's begin with:

1 John 2:15-17 (NASB) *Do not love the world nor the things in the world. If anyone loves the world, the love of the Father is not in him. [16] For all that is in the world, the lust of the flesh and the lust of the eyes and the boastful pride of life, is not from the Father, but is from the world. [17] The world is passing away, and also its lusts; but the one who does the will of God lives forever.*

"World" in these three verses is represented by that which is offered by the five senses in which we temporarily live. The Greek work is "kosmos." K. S. Wuest, a Greek scholar comments on its usage in this way:

Kosmos (Κοσμος) refers to an ordered system. Here it is the ordered system of which Satan is the head, his fallen angels and demons are his emissaries, and the unsaved of the human race are his subjects, together with those purposes, pursuits,

45

pleasures, practices, and places where God is not wanted. Much in this world-system is religious, cultured, refined, and intellectual. But it is anti-God and anti-Christ.[2]

This ordered system, our cultural and educational training, teaches us that we are the master of our own souls, we are in command, and we must satisfy ourselves! This is a lie, from the "father of lies," and will lead to ruin. **You have already tasted this ruin**, this insanity, if you struggle with unwanted habits and addictions. John says do not "love" the world or anything in it. God certainly gave us much in his creation to enjoy, but not to love, our love is to be reserved for him, and those who he gives us to love. John continues to define loving the world and the things therein:

- The lust of the eyes (that which we see – we want) i.e. **things** we think will make us happy, will fulfill. **Material things** (stuff of the world) and **immaterial things** (women and men relationships, friends, etc.)
- The lust of the flesh (appetites of our bodies) i.e. food, drink, smoke, sex, drugs, gambling, adrenaline rush, all kinds of practices and perversions outside of God-ordained marriage, exercise (extremes), sleep (extremes), etc.
- The boastful pride of life (fame and fortune) i.e. seeking recognition, promotion, elevation (in people's eyes), amassed monies, power and anything which promotes pride, etc.

These things are not from God, but from the world system, THEY WILL NOT, CANNOT fill up the emptiness of your soul! To love these things is to forsake God and his love. John concludes this passage; the world (all the pseudo-pleasures) is passing away, but the one who does the will of God (lives by God's good provision and rule) lives forever! (Not merely exists or gets by, but LIVES FULLY).

HONEST QUESTIONS LEADING TO FREEDOM

1. Do you agree that what you have been doing to fill your emptiness is NOT WORKING?

2. Will you confess this (Say it out loud to God, yourself, and others)?

3. Will you reject "the world" as described, not relying on it to fill you?

4. Will you submit to God (invite him to fill you, trust him, seek him)?

Notes and Thoughts:

CHAPTER 8
WHAT FILLS? WHAT SATISFIES?

John 10:10 (NLT) *The thief's purpose is to steal and kill and destroy. My purpose is to give them a rich and satisfying life.*

The Psalmist proclaims the design and ability of the Almighty God in

Psalm 103:1-5 *Praise the LORD, O my soul; all my inmost being, praise his holy name. Praise the LORD, O my soul, and forget not all his benefits— ³who forgives all your sins and heals all your diseases, ⁴who redeems your life from the pit and crowns you with love and compassion, who satisfies your desires with good things so that your youth is renewed like the eagle's.*

Here the Psalmist instructs his soul (mind, will, and emotions) to praise the Lord! This is a good habit to acquire, to include God in all things every day. Soul; do not forget God's benefits, he forgives and heals (makes whole and sets free). Soul; God crowns you (puts importance on your head) with love (relationship with himself and others) and compassion. Soul; God SATISFIES YOUR DESIRES WITH GOOD THINGS so that you have the energy to fly (soar above the pain and anguish and emptiness of this world)! How awesome if this were so? **IT IS SO!** But you must be satisfied with HIS provision!

God establishes relationships, first, for us to know him and him us. **John 10:14** *"I am the good shepherd; I know my sheep and my sheep know me*—Jesus uses figurative language here, he is speaking about people, not sheep. Notice the adjective "good" before shepherd. It is most comforting to know that the "good" shepherd knows me and I can know him! This implies a relationship. A relationship requires communication to be effective. This communication must move in both directions; from us to God and from God to us. It cannot be effective as a static communication but must be dynamic. What I mean by this is that texting can only communicate a bare minimum between lovers. Dynamic communication can be exemplified by a conversation that includes substantial interaction. Terms of endearment, honesty about needs, struggles, and difficulties; there must also be laughter and joy and pleasure shared between them for a real relationship to flourish. God desires for us to speak our hearts to him. He wishes for our prayers to be spoken to him as a person who loves and cares for us, not as a God who is far from us and has never had "skin." (Jesus had skin. He experienced feelings and temptations and emotions and thoughts and love and joy and laughter.) What is most surprising is that God <u>wants</u> to speak to us!

Hebrews 1:1-2 *In the past God spoke to our forefathers through the prophets at many times and in various ways, ² but in these last days he has spoken to us by his Son, whom he appointed heir of all things, and through whom he made the universe.* We see God move from speaking through human beings in very restrictive ways to speaking to us directly. Jesus is God and Jesus is human, a great mystery but nonetheless true. Jesus' Spirit comes to live in everyone who believes in him and he speaks to our spirits. **Romans 8:16** *The Spirit himself testifies with our spirit that we are God's children.* The Spirit of God speaks with our spirit. He tells us we are children of God, personally, individually. He tells us much more!

> **John 16:13-15** *But when he, the Spirit of truth, comes, he will guide you into all truth. He will not speak on his own; he will speak only what he hears, and he will tell you what is yet to come. ¹⁴ He will bring glory to me by taking from what is mine*

and making it known to you. ¹⁵ *All that belongs to the Father is mine. That is why I said the Spirit will take from what is mine and make it known to you.*

Jesus spoke these words personally and intimately to the disciples after he washed their feet ... and before he went to the cross. The Holy Spirit speaks to us! He guides, he leads, he convicts, he comforts, he teaches us in personal (person to person) and intimate (speaking to our inmost being) ways. He tells us exactly what we need to know, when we need to know it. We only need to be listening! **John 10:27** *My sheep listen to my voice; I know them, and they follow me.* Listening to God will fill our bottomless pit of relationship; to know that he cares enough to converse with us, listen to us, and speak to us is most fulfilling. He speaks to us through his Spirit and through his Word. The Scriptures are an important means for God to speak with you and like listening it only takes reading them and allowing him to speak through his written words to you.

God also provides relationship with others to fill your emptiness. He places people in your life to love, confide in, listen to, laugh with, for accountability, and to live life with. From the intimacy of the marriage of two individuals to the friendship around a fire-pit or coffee shop; fellowship is God's design to satisfy our insatiable desire for relationship. Family is a word the Bible uses to tell us of this relationship in which he has called us to live. God himself lives in relationship within the Godhead and he has intended for us to live the same way. This is his plan to fill the bottomless pit of relationship within our souls. **He fills it with his infinite self and his finite people**; both are necessary to live free in this life. When we are drinking of the living water he fills us. The "stuff" he uses is relationship with him and fellowship with others. These are crucial to live free of the addictiveness of our past! We need help! God has provided for us to find it. **Ephesians** 1:4-5 *For he chose us in him before the creation of the world to be holy and blameless in his sight. In love* ⁵ *he predestined us to be adopted as his sons through Jesus Christ, in accordance with his pleasure and will—* God chose US in Jesus before time began that we might become holy and blameless. This comes about because of our relationship with Jesus the perfect man. In love he planned for us to be in his family, sons and daughters, intimately related, loving and helping each other. He did this because it gives him pleasure! It is God's will!

> **Psalm 133** *How good and pleasant it is when brothers live together in unity! It is like precious oil poured on the head, running down on the beard, running down on Aaron's beard, down upon the collar of his robes.* *³It is as if the dew of Hermon were falling on Mount Zion. For there the* LORD *bestows his blessing, even life forevermore.*

This Psalm has much in it but read it again and <u>feel</u> the pleasure of the Lord within it; it is marvelous. God loves to bestow the blessing of Life on his children. He makes us free of that which keeps us from him so that we may enjoy him forever. When we fellowship with each other (dare to confess our sin, fear, failure, and progress) we are then able not only have others help carry our burdens (**Galatians 6:2** *Carry each other's burdens, and in this way you will fulfill the law of Christ.*), but be able to comfort others who find themselves in similar bondage. **2 Corinthians 1:3-4** *Praise be to the God and Father of our Lord Jesus Christ, the Father of compassion and the God of all comfort,* *⁴ who comforts us in all our troubles, so that we can comfort those in any trouble with the comfort we ourselves have received from God.* Here we see the Apostle Paul praising God for all his comfort! In all our troubles from (specific difficulties, in our case unwanted habits and addictive behaviors) we may comfort those of our brothers and sisters in ANY trouble. The troubles may be different but the constant is that HE IS THE GOD OF COMFORT! Once we have experienced his comfort, liberation and victory we may give hope and help to others in their difficulties. If you are caught in an addiction today DO NOT DESPAIR! Others have been there and been set free! As unbelievable as it may seem to you today you will be able to help others find the "Father of all compassion and the God of all comfort." This is possible because the bottomless pit of relationship is filled with the infinite God and his design through finite brothers and sisters. This is liberation!

God establishes significance for every individual. God has purpose for you, a plan for you! He has established for you substantial work to do in his kingdom. God's desire for you is to contribute; not to try to fill yourself, attempting to satisfy the "lust of the eyes, the lust of the flesh and the boastful pride of life" (**1 John 2:16**). We know that pursuing these things does not fill our emptiness, we have tried it over and over and it inevitably fails! Two Proverbs come to mind, the first is **Proverbs 16:9** *In his heart a man plans his course, but the LORD determines his steps.* For the one belonging to God, God corrects his path. In our application we may find ourselves in bondage to addictive behavior, we have chosen our course, but God determines your steps. He has something, most likely many things he desires for you to accomplish. All we have done has led to more and more emptiness, the fulfilling thing is to do what God purposes. The second is **Proverbs 20:24** *A man's steps are directed by the LORD. How then can anyone understand his own way?* Have you never wondered, "Why do I continue to do this (supply your behavior, habit, or addiction)?" It is because you are trying to understand how to fill up the insatiable pits in your life. When you are in this condition you **cannot** fathom the magnitude of this bottomless pit, let alone the hopelessness of trying to fill it. It is like trying to fill the Grand Canyon with sand using a teaspoon, though that may even be possible given enough time. But when the Lord directs your steps; he is all-knowing, he is all-powerful. He knows what will fill you, he is able to help you accomplish it; not only this, HE WANTS TO DO IT! The work that God gives us to do is not easy, not safe, not always joyful, certainly not always simple (pick up "a" glue it to "b" and you have made "c"), but it is always fulfilling! It is always pleasing to him! It is always significant, because it is always Kingdom work. It has eternal value.

For those of us who struggle with addictive behavior this verse of Scripture is particularly hard-hitting. It comes from

> **John 3:19-21** *This is the verdict: Light has come into the world, but men loved darkness instead of light because their deeds were evil. [20] Everyone who does evil hates the light, and will not come into the light for fear that his deeds will be exposed. [21] But whoever lives by the truth comes into the light, so that it may be seen plainly that what he has done has been done through God."*

The conclusion is that when we are partaking of our addictive behavior we DO NOT WANT IT EXPOSED! That which we use, attempting to fill our emptiness is shameful to us because God, who loves us, convicts us by his Spirit. When we turn to God to fill us and we worship him by our actions, deeds, work; we love to have our work examined. This kind of work pleases God and we are proud of it. It is clean work. It is holy work. It is honorable work.

> *2 Timothy 2:20-21 Now in a great house there are not only vessels of gold and silver but also of wood and clay, some for honorable use, some for dishonorable. ²¹ Therefore, if anyone cleanses himself from what is dishonorable, he will be a vessel for honorable use, set apart as holy, useful to the master of the house, ready for every good work.*

Verse 21 is what we are about in this book. Being cleansed from "dishonorable" behavior and becoming useful to Jesus; ready to do work that is worthy. The worthy work of God will fill our emptiness. The purpose to which God sets us is always consuming our emptiness.

Romans 8:28 *And we know that in all things God works for the good of those who love him, who have been called according to his purpose.* We have been called to fulfill the purposes of God! This happens in great and small ways. When we love God (more than our idols, our addictions) and we desire to do his will, God works in all things on our behalf for GOOD! Make all the money you can, buy all the toys you want, get the job of your dreams, have everything go your way, you will still be empty, hungering for more. This emptiness drives us toward our habits and addictive behaviors. But God has a different plan for you. Hear what the Psalmist say declares:

Psalm 107:4-9
*⁴ Some wandered in desert wastelands,
finding no way to a city where they could settle.
⁵ They were hungry and thirsty,*

and their lives ebbed away.
6 Then they cried out to the LORD in their trouble,
and he delivered them from their distress.
7 He led them by a straight way
to a city where they could settle.
8 Let them give thanks to the LORD for his unfailing love
and his wonderful deeds for men,
9 for he satisfies the thirsty
and fills the hungry with good things.

Now we who struggle with addictive behaviors understand right well what wandering in desert wastelands is like. Of course, the Psalmist is speaking of Israel in the desert, but we can apply it to our desert, the waste of our lives in habits and addictions. They were hungry and thirsty, nothing would satisfy them and their lives ebbed away. Have you ever felt like this? Then in a moment of sanity they cried out to the Lord in their trouble (struggle), and he HEARD THEM! He delivered them from their distress! He led them to safety and productivity; they praised him and kept praising their deliverer because he SATISFIES THE THIRSTY AND FILLS THE HUNGRY WITH GOOD THINGS!

NOW GET READY FOR SOMETHING AWESOME!

Ephesians 2:10 *For we are God's workmanship, created in Christ Jesus to do good works, which God prepared in advance for us to do.* God made us: Unique. Everyone is one of a kind. Then, he re-created us in Jesus (gave us a rebirth). Why? To do good works! These good works that we are to do; God prepared long before we came on the scene. These good works are tailor-made for your uniqueness! These good works are not random; they are specially customized, personalized for you! As you do them, they will fill your bottomless pit for purpose. Nothing else will satisfy you. **Matthew 5:6** *Blessed are those who hunger and thirst for righteousness, for they will be filled.* When we hunger and thirst for righteousness, God's righteous work for us to do, our hunger and thirst (bottomless pit) gets filled. In other words, when we stop being hungry for the things that do not satisfy, and cease thirsting for that which is not good (stop looking for our habits and addictions to satisfy us), then God reveals our purpose and fills us to overflowing! From **Psalm 23:6** *You prepare a table before me in the presence of my enemies. You anoint my head with oil; my cup overflows.* We see that the enemies, in our case, our addictions become vanquished and God feeds us with his good works right in front of them and we overflow with significance. Let me conclude this section with these great words from Paul to the church at Colossae.

> **Colossians 1:10-14** *And we pray this in order that you may live a life worthy of the Lord and may please him in every way: bearing fruit in every good work, growing in the knowledge of God, [11] being strengthened with all power according to his glorious might so that you may have great endurance and patience, and joyfully [12] giving thanks to the Father, who has qualified you to share in the inheritance of the saints in the kingdom of light. [13] For he has rescued us from the dominion of darkness and brought us into the kingdom of the Son he loves, [14] in whom we have redemption, the forgiveness of sins.*

Most of this book is written to those struggling with addictive behaviors, but some are reading it who have been set free from their addictions. To these I would include these words from Deuteronomy:

> **Deuteronomy 8:10-14** *When you have eaten and are satisfied, praise the LORD your God for the good land he has given you. [11] Be careful that you do not forget the LORD your God, failing to observe his commands, his laws and his decrees that I am giving you this day. [12] Otherwise, when you eat and are satisfied, when you build fine houses and settle down, [13] and when your herds and flocks grow large and your silver and gold increase and all you have is multiplied, [14] then your heart will become proud and you will forget the LORD your God, who brought you out of Egypt, out of the land of slavery.*

This admonition is for those "brought out of slavery," the temptation to "settle down," is grave. Reread it, it is a challenge to continue to allow the infinite God and his finite people to fill your pit of relationship. It is a challenge to continue to walk in his purpose and be fulfilled with his significance.

HONEST QUESTIONS LEADING TO FREEDOM

1. What resonated with you in this chapter? What hit you hard? (You may need to read it again)

2. With what truth in this chapter do you struggle?

3. What are you going to do about it?

Notes and Thoughts:

CHAPTER 9
THE WAY OUT

What practical things can we do to become liberated? How do we go about realistically filling our souls? There are three actions we can take to facilitate freedom from our habitual and addictive behaviors. One, a renewed mind, two, a changed heart, three, is full disclosure.

First, a RENEWED MIND is needed to be free. We must change our thinking.

> **Romans 12:1-2** *Therefore, I urge you, brothers, in view of God's mercy, to offer your bodies as living sacrifices, holy and pleasing to God—this is your spiritual act of worship.* [2] *Do not conform any longer to the pattern of this world, but be transformed by the renewing of your mind. Then you will be able to test and approve what God's will is—his good, pleasing and perfect will.*

Worshiping God by giving him your body is directly related to habitual and addictive behavior. All the parts of your body! Stomach, hands, mouth, private parts, all of it belongs to God and we worship him when we surrender our bodies to his purpose. The "world" has taught us to think in certain ways. The ways of the world are not God's ways. Our culture, our educational systems, our morals and ethics, when formed by men of the world will not produce in us the results of godliness. But when we begin to think according to God's principles, his morality, his ethics, his statutes, commands, decrees, precepts, and truths we are transformed. This word "transformed" means to "change in character or condition." When we change our thinking i.e. how we think about God and what he is doing in our lives, how he wants to fill our empty souls; then we see our behavior change. Jesus said, *"Clean the inside of the cup and dish and then the outside will also be clean."* (**Matthew 23:26**) What he means by this is that when we will clean the inside of ourselves, our thinking, our faith, our intentions, then the outside, our behavior, the things people observe, our actions will be clean also. Another way of saying this is found in **Mark 2:22** *And no one pours new wine into old wineskins. If he does, the wine will burst the skins, and both the wine and the wineskins will be ruined. No, he pours new wine into new wineskins."* The new wine of your renewed mind (new thinking about what really satisfies) will burst the old wineskin of your addictive behaviors and unwanted habits. We need new behaviors, good, holy, pleasing behaviors that are the result of new thinking. Thus, the last of Romans 12:2 … *Then you will be able to test and approve what God's will is—his good, pleasing and perfect will.* The change comes from the inside, allowing God to fill us to overflowing with his LIFE, his love, his words, his thoughts, and his purpose. This changes the way we live!

This principle of a renewed inside changing the outside is found throughout the Scriptures. One famous passage is found in

Proverbs 3:5-8
⁵ Trust in the LORD with all your heart
and lean not on your own understanding;
⁶ in all your ways acknowledge him,
and he will make your paths straight.
⁷ Do not be wise in your own eyes;
fear the LORD and shun evil.
⁸ This will bring health to your body
and nourishment to your bones.

Trusting in the Lord with all your heart and not leaning on your own thinking implies a renewed mind. "In all your ways" means in all your attitude, planning and action; acknowledge God. As a result, he makes your path straight, this suggests action without wavering, hesitating or veering off into impure, unclean, habitual and addictive behavior. When we think we are being wise or astute we probably need to seek counsel from some godly person. The gaining of wisdom often requires wise counsel, first from God (his Spirit and Word) and from people who are more mature than we. Once true wisdom is gained (not the kind we find in ourselves which is often foolish) it brings about fear (reverence) of the Lord and we avoid evil. The Psalmist ends by saying if we change our thinking (renew our minds) in these ways it brings "health to your body and nourishment to your bones."

> **Ephesians 4:17-24** *So I tell you this, and insist on it in the Lord, that you must no longer live as the Gentiles do, in the futility of their thinking. [18] They are darkened in their understanding and separated from the life of God because of the ignorance that is in them due to the hardening of their hearts. [19] Having lost all sensitivity, they have given themselves over to sensuality so as to indulge in every kind of impurity, with a continual lust for more. [20] You, however, did not come to know Christ that way. [21] Surely you heard of him and were taught in him in accordance with the truth that is in Jesus. [22] You were taught, with regard to your former way of life, to put off your old self, which is being corrupted by its deceitful desires; [23] to be made new in the attitude of your minds; [24] and to put on the new self, created to be like God in true righteousness and holiness.*

In this passage "the gentiles" are those who are unbelievers, those without faith. We see that they have a lifestyle that does not include God. This thinking is termed "futile" and "dark" resulting in separation from God because their hearts (souls) are hardened toward him. This is the case with most people with addictive behavior. They try and try and try to fill up their empty, bottomless pits of relationship and purpose with their own inventions, and then they invent some more. All the time they are getting more and more and more bitter about how life is working out and they become hardened in their hearts, believing that all is lost and "I will never be free and good." The passage continues, *[19] Having lost all sensitivity, they have given themselves over to sensuality so as to indulge in every kind of impurity, with a continual lust for more.* Losing all sensitivity toward God and godliness they quit! Not wanting to deal with difficult lives; they give up hope and just go for whatever temporarily satisfies and then do it again. DO NOT LET THIS BE YOU!

Those of us who trust in God and believe in the renewing nature of Jesus Christ are able to see things differently. We can THINK from a hopeful perspective. We can KNOW the power of God to save us from our slavery. We must learn to "put off" this futile, ineffective, pointless "old self." That is who we are in our habits and addiction(s). This "old self" is being corrupted by the deceitful desires. Deceitful desires are those cravings for relationship and purpose that promise to be filled by our habits and addictions, but being deceitful it is all a lie. These can never satisfy us. It is somewhat like sucking on a pacifier, it gives you the illusion of security.

Rather, *[23] to be made new in the attitude of your minds;* this is the "renewed mind" we have been talking about. The new way of thinking, believing that God is able to change us, fill us, love us! We are to "put on" this new self, *created to be like God in true righteousness and holiness.* Wow! God created me to be like him in true righteousness and holiness? Then he must make a way for me to be able to actually do it!

In addition, A CHANGE OF HEART is needed. In this portion we will look at our emotions.

> **Luke 7:36-50** *Now one of the Pharisees invited Jesus to have dinner with him, so he went to the Pharisee's house and reclined at the table. [37] When a woman who had lived a sinful life in that town learned that Jesus was eating at the Pharisee's house, she brought an alabaster jar of perfume, [38] and as she stood behind him at his feet weeping, she began to wet his feet with her tears. Then she wiped them with her hair, kissed them and poured perfume on them. [39] When the Pharisee who had invited him saw this, he said to himself, "If this man were a prophet, he would*

know who is touching him and what kind of woman she is—that she is a sinner." [40] Jesus answered him, "Simon, I have something to tell you." "Tell me, teacher," he said.[41] "Two men owed money to a certain moneylender. One owed him five hundred denarii, and the other fifty. [42] Neither of them had the money to pay him back, so he canceled the debts of both. Now which of them will love him more?" [43] Simon replied, "I suppose the one who had the bigger debt canceled.""You have judged correctly," Jesus said. [44] Then he turned toward the woman and said to Simon, "Do you see this woman? I came into your house. You did not give me any water for my feet, but she wet my feet with her tears and wiped them with her hair. [45] You did not give me a kiss, but this woman, from the time I entered, has not stopped kissing my feet. [46] You did not put oil on my head, but she has poured perfume on my feet. [47] Therefore, I tell you, her many sins have been forgiven—for she loved much. But he who has been forgiven little loves little." [48] Then Jesus said to her, "Your sins are forgiven." [49] The other guests began to say among themselves, "Who is this who even forgives sins?" [50] Jesus said to the woman, "Your faith has saved you; go in peace."

Simon, a Pharisee (religious ruler) invited Jesus and many guests to his house for dinner. He neglected the proper etiquette, at least with Jesus. A woman, known to be a notorious sinner, with an alabaster jar of costly perfume crashed the party. (Alabaster was a substance that was very expensive, a sealed jar that had to be destroyed to obtain the costly substance from inside.) She stood behind Jesus and was weeping, when she saw that her tears were falling on Jesus' feet she knelt before him and dried his feet with her hair. She then took the jar (perhaps her whole earthly wealth) and broke it and anointed Jesus feet with the costly perfume. Simon, the Pharisee was watching with a critical eye and making a judgment not only on the woman, who was well-known, but on Jesus. Jesus then, tells a story of two men who owed a debt they could not pay. One owed a little and the other a lot. Jesus asked Simon which of them loved the man who had forgiven him more? The one who owed more, answered Simon. He was correct. Jesus told Simon, what he had not done, and what the woman had done, that she had loved him with everything she had! She had loved him much! Jesus forgave her all of her sins and she had peace with God. Her heart was changed in that moment. **Matthew 6:21** *For where your treasure is, there your heart will be also.* She wanted to love Jesus more than she wanted what her sin had purchased for her (the costly jar of perfume). Jesus became her treasure. The New Testament implies that she never went back to her addiction! She had found the true source of Life, the spring of living water. She found relationship with Jesus and his disciples (yes, there were women disciples following Jesus) and she found purpose in serving him and others.

HONEST QUESTIONS LEADING TO FREEDOM

1. How must our thinking be changed to promote freedom?

2. What impact did the explanation of Romans 12:1-2 have on you?

3. List some ways your thinking has been "futile?"

4. What did you learn from the story of the sinful woman who crashed the Pharisee's party?

IT TAKES A HEART CHANGE!

Matthew 13:15 quotes **Isaiah 6:9** *For this people's heart has become calloused; they hardly hear with their ears, and they have closed their eyes. Otherwise they might see with their eyes, hear with their ears, understand with their hearts and turn, and I would heal them.'*

We who suffer from addictive behavior(s) have or have had calloused hearts. We know what it is like to hear friends and family, people who love us, give us advice and yet pay no attention to it. We have closed our eyes and ears. But if we "turn" and look and listen we see God, we see his forgiveness through Jesus, his power through his Spirit to deliver us and heal us. It takes a heart change! **Hebrews 3:12-13** *See to it, brothers, that none of you has a sinful, unbelieving heart that turns away from the living God.* [13] *But encourage one another daily, as long as it is called Today, so that none of you may be hardened by sin's deceitfulness.* When we are in relationship with godly people and with Jesus, we may be encouraged through this relationship into freedom and productivity. It takes a heart change!

Third, FULL DISCLOSURE is needed. "The truth and nothing but the truth." And all of it! When Adam and Eve were naked and not ashamed, there was nothing hidden. Their souls were as bare as their bodies. Then, first, they entertained hidden motives, hidden desires, hidden hungers, etc. As people who struggle with habits and addiction(s) we are not inexperienced with deception, lies, dishonesty, fabrication, half-truths, pretense, cheating, duplicity, posturing and many more disreputable behaviors. Most of them used to hide or cover up our addictive strategies. We will use almost anything to keep from being exposed. This illustration may be somewhat crass but it is effective; when you have eaten something disagreeable and your stomach begins to turn over, you <u>know</u> that after you vomit you will feel better, so you do the only smart thing, you do everything possible <u>NOT</u> to throw up! This describes the individual who knows he needs help, he is dependent, addicted, knows where the help is, but refuses to confess (recognize) and surrender. God knows all about it! As we have said before, HE ALREADY

KNOWS, you cannot hide it from HIM. Hold up the mirror; admit to yourself that you need help; find a committed friend and FULLY DISCLOSE.

The church at Ephesus was having difficulty with people's hidden sin and hidden motives. An event happened and the result is reported in

> **Acts 19:18-20** *Many of those who believed now came and openly confessed their evil deeds.[19] A number who had practiced sorcery brought their scrolls together and burned them publicly. When they calculated the value of the scrolls, the total came to fifty thousand drachmas. [20] In this way the word of the Lord spread widely and grew in power.*

Sorcery or magic was what they used to have power over others (the boastful pride of life), they were addicted to filling their bottomless pits of relationship and purpose by manipulating others. When they heard the truth about Jesus coming to free them from the BONDAGE of their sinful behavior they publicly brought these very expensive and rare scrolls of evil and burned them. They fully disclosed their past and proclaimed a new FUTURE OF FREEDOM. Liberation from what could not fill them was worth more than guilt, shame, and exposure!

> E. A. Griffin writes:
> A well-known fact of sharing is called the bus-rider phenomenon. People often prefer to bare their soul to a stranger rather than to a lifelong friend. The reason is obvious. I'll probably never see my Greyhound seatmate again, so there's no risk in sharing my innermost hopes and fears. Although this kind of self-disclosure affords a degree of catharsis—getting things off our chest—it doesn't give us any of the interpersonal benefits listed earlier. Besides, it's risky. How do we know that person isn't a friend of a friend? Often the temporary relief of "letting it all hang out" to a stranger is overshadowed by doubts and embarrassment the morning after. It's much more satisfying to select a listener with whom we have an ongoing relationship.
> I'm fortunate to have my pastor as my best friend. We've been

close for ten years. Every week we'll spend an hour and a half in the steam room at the local YMCA. The continuing nature of our friendship means that the intimate details of my life that swirl together with the vapor are heard in the context of mutual responsibility to each other. He's lucky too. Although I'm active in the youth program of our church, I don't serve as an elder or deacon. My only assignment is this unofficial "steam room committee." He can use me as a confessor, cheerleader or sounding board for ideas. Because we have a history of many soggy hours together, neither of us feels "on stage" with each other.

My wife and I have experienced this same accountability with other couples at a marriage retreat. Six couples shared struggles of faith, vocation, sex, money, conflict and parenting between themselves and among each other. Self-disclosure wasn't cheap. Material shared would still be known by those important to us a week later. It placed an emphasis on authenticity.[1]

Griffin's story is common among "freed" believers in Christ, those who have had Jesus break their chains. We need help in remaining free! Jesus came to free us and give us abundant life but life in this world is difficult. All of us who struggle with habitual and addictive behaviors know our triggers (more about triggers in the next section). These triggers cause us to stumble and eventually fall. We need confessors, people we can trust, people who will speak the truth to us, people who will not judge us but hold us accountable to that which we have committed; namely to be FREE IN CHRIST JESUS! It is amazing what simply fully disclosing our temptations and thoughts, exposing them to someone else, can do to set us right again. **Ecclesiastes 4:9-10** *Two are better than one, because they have a good return for their work: [10]If one falls down, his friend can help him up. But pity the man who falls and has no one to help him up!* All of us, everyone, needs people who know all about us. If you are married I highly suggest your mate. Full disclosure with your life-partner is most rewarding. Men need men to understand men, also. Ask any man (or woman) if they understand the opposite gender, you will find here a mystery, a God mystery. It keeps life interesting. So, lifemates are good to have as confessors on both sides, but men need men and women need women. Full disclosure of your life demands trust, intimacy, and lack of judgment, genuine encouragement and availability. I recommend face to face disclosure. Phones, texting, computer-talk and all the rest are useful, but nothing can compare to the intimacy of one to one face time.

One of the most candid and refreshing promises in the Scripture is found in **James 5:16** *Therefore confess your sins to each other and pray for each other so that you may be healed.* The verb tense in the original language indicates that this is an on-going confession and prayer. This shows the need for confession of our lives and prayer for each other which brings healing. This healing could be physical, mental (the way we think), emotional (the way we feel) or a healing of our will (becoming willing to follow in right ways), or spiritual (getting God's perspective). For the purposes of this book and addictiveness we might say it this way: If you truly want to be healed, confess to each other fully and pray for each other continually. (The author has found this full disclosure to be profound in his own healing and practices it regularly.)

HEALING QUESTIONS LEADING TO FREEDOM

1. Have you ever fully disclosed to anyone?

2. To whom could you choose to be fully disclosed? List some people.

Notes and Thoughts:

F. Michael Grubbs

PART 3 LIVING FREE

CHAPTER 10
FITS AND STARTS

This chapter is about what to expect as you begin living free. Fits and starts means that most of you will have success for some, usually short, period of time. Enough to make you think you have the habit conquered. What commonly happens next is that you will fail, return to your habit and begin to "beat yourself up," for your weakness, frailty, incompetence, etc. This is called a "fit." After you have come to yourself, you will remember that you got into the habit or addiction over some period of time and it will take some period of time to fully master yourself in this dimension (not that you have permission to fail, YOU DO NOT!). Your fellowship, the people with whom you are in relationship and the ones you fully disclose with should be firm, but kind and help you back onto the road to recovery. This is called a "start." (The reader should know that these are the author's terms, not commonly recognized by other counselors.) The number of fits and starts you will experience depends on you, the depth of your relationship with Jesus and your desire to be a God-pleaser. God, the Holy Spirit is your helper and the one who convicts you of sin in your life, he is also your comforter and reminder that you are forgiven and that God has something better planned for you.

The Apostle Paul, as well as all believers, experienced fits and starts in overcoming his difficulties.

Romans 7:21- 8:2 (NLT) *I have discovered this principle of* *life—that when I want to do what is right, I inevitably do what is wrong. ²²I love God's law with all my heart. ²³But there is another power within me that is at war with my mind. This power makes me a slave to the sin that is still within me.²⁴Oh, what a miserable person I am! Who will free me from this life that is dominated by sin and death?²⁵Thank God! The answer is in Jesus Christ our Lord. So you see how it is: In my mind I really want to obey God's law, but because of my sinful nature I am a slave to sin. 8 So now there is no condemnation for those who belong to Christ Jesus. ²And because you belong to him, the power of the life-giving Spirit has freed you from the power of sin that leads to death.*

What Paul is saying to the Roman church and to all of us is that overcoming our sinful nature is not simple or easy! It took the WORD OF GOD, Jesus, TO BECOME FLESH, TO LIVE FULLY AS A MAN, TO DIE AS A PERFECT SACRIFICE, AND TO RISE FROM THE DEAD to accomplish it. Then, God, the Holy Spirit works throughout our lives to make us holy to transform us, so that we may live eternally with him; holy, spotless, blameless and productive. Paul also said that **the battle is fought in the mind**, our decision-making part. We are free to decide to be a God-pleasing person, free from that which once enslaved us. We are free to choose our habitual sin, also. As we begin to take our decision seriously and more seriously we make more and more right decisions and God's grace teaches us to say "NO" to our sinful behaviors. **Titus 2:11-12** *For the grace of God that brings salvation has appeared to all men. ¹²It teaches us to say "No" to ungodliness and worldly passions, and to live self-controlled, upright and godly lives in this present age,.* So that we are as **Romans 8:1-2** above says, free from the power of sin that leads to death! BUT WE MUST CHOOSE! Not just once but every day, every time of temptation, in every moment of weakness. The key is that when we fail, not to turn it into a pity party, which throws us, further into "giving up mode," but to recognize it for what it is, A FAILURE. Confess it, disclose it fully, and turn from it again with all the strength that God gives you. The telephone, especially the cell phone is a wonderful aid. When tempted make the call

BEFORE YOU FAIL. Get God's encouragement through the people he has given you to live life with. Be there for them also when they need to call you!

> **James 1:13-15** *When tempted, no one should say, "God is tempting me." For God cannot be tempted by evil, nor does he tempt anyone; ¹⁴ but each one is tempted when, by his own evil desire, he is dragged away and enticed. ¹⁵ Then, after desire has conceived, it gives birth to sin; and sin, when it is full-grown, gives birth to death.*

The temptation itself is **not** sin. Notice the "when," in verse 14; this IS going to happen! The stopping point is "being dragged away and enticed." This is where we need HELP! We need not only to pray, but to make the strengthening call to the people we trust.

> **Hebrews 10:24** *And let us consider how we may spur one another on toward love and good deeds.*

Fits and starts are to be expected. I cannot say this strong enough; A FAILURE IS NOT AN EXCUSE, REASON, EXPLANATION, or DEFENSE for sinful behaviors. If we fail, we are to immediately despise the sin, confess i.e. fully disclosing what happened and marking our temptation and enticement, recognizing it for what it is and re-commit to free living.

James 4:7-10 *So humble yourselves before God. Resist the devil, and he will flee from you. ⁸ Come close to God, and God will come close to you. Wash your hands, you sinners; purify your hearts, for your loyalty is divided between God and the world. ⁹ Let there be tears for what you have done. Let there be sorrow and deep grief. Let there be sadness instead of laughter, and gloom instead of joy. ¹⁰ Humble yourselves before the Lord, and he will lift you up in honor.* James, in this passage describes the right response to a "fit:" humility, approaching God with confession, washing (fully disclosing), and grieving for sinful action constitutes the right response to a fit. And when we have humbled ourselves before the Lord he will lift us up for honor. This is a "start!" Our "posse," those who will walk with us through life, those who are committed to living life with us, are invaluable for the process of LIVING FREE.

HONEST QUESTIONS LEADING TO FREEDOM

1. What is a "fit?"

2. Describe your last "fit", how did you handle it?

3. What is a "start?"

4. Who is in your "posse?"

5. Are you committed to fully disclose to them?

Notes and Thoughts:

CHAPTER 11
IDENTIFYING TRIGGERS

A crucial, vital tool to understanding our habitual or addictive behavior is "the trigger." A trigger can be anything; a sight, a smell, a sound, down-time (with nothing to do), a thought, a word, a song, a place, most anything that brings on the temptation. Recognizing these triggers is fundamental to LIVING FREE. As we discussed in the first section of this book habits are formed when we react to certain stimuli in the same fashion over and over again. It is a behavioral response. So, when you are attempting to live free of that behavior, when the stimulus appears YOU MUST ACT DIFFERENTLY! Here is an example used previously: "For instance, I may be feeling upset with my boss at work for a poor performance evaluation, which I do not think I deserve, the abyss in my soul for significance begins to act up and I need to feel good about myself. My "go to" action is chocolate (substitute your preference here) so I go to the cupboard and eat half of a pound of Cadbury. This makes me feel better so the next time and the next time again I turn to chocolate for gratification." In this example the individual is drinking birdbath water (trying to fill his bottomless pit for purpose) instead of going to the Living Water. How do you get to the living water? One answer is prayer. "But when I get like that I can't pray" you might say. Call one of your posse to pray with you, spend some time in the Scriptures, have a coffee with your "confessor" and speak out your temptation. These things seem simple and they are, BUT THEY WORK!

Instead of turning to the things of the world that temporarily, briefly give some satisfaction then leave you in the ashes, you are turning to the God-given, holy gifts to overcome the habits/addictions.

> **James 1:2-8** (NLT) *Dear brothers and sisters, when troubles come your way, consider it an opportunity for great joy. ³ For you know that when your faith is tested, your endurance has a chance to grow. ⁴ So let it grow, for when your endurance is fully developed, you will be perfect and complete, needing nothing. ⁵ If you need wisdom, ask our generous God, and he will give it to you. He will not rebuke you for asking. ⁶ But when you ask him, be sure that your faith is in God alone. Do not waver, for a person with divided loyalty is as unsettled as a wave of the sea that is blown and tossed by the wind. ⁷ Such people should not expect to receive anything from the Lord. ⁸ Their loyalty is divided between God and the world, and they are unstable in everything they do.*

Here is an explanation for the process of living free and a warning about the help God will provide.

First, troubles (hardships, tests, temptations, enticements, difficulties, stresses, quandaries, suffering, adversity, struggles, and etc. come to us for a reason! To give us an opportunity for great joy! When God proves himself faithful, and friends prove themselves faithful, faith is formed and matured. Endurance grows; bigger tests and more maturity are before you (remember this is a lifetime process and there are many people behind you that will need your maturity in the future). The end result is wholeness, needing nothing (that is, you have found Jesus and his kingdom to be all you need). In the meantime, we need WISDOM, these are the what, how, when, where of the questions of life; we are instructed to ASK GOD and he will give it to you. This wisdom may come by many avenues; Scripture, the Holy Spirit's revelation, wise counsel from mature men and women, something you read, even something someone says, etc. but be assured God will provide the wisdom we seek.

Second, the warning is that you seek wisdom in God alone!

The world's wisdom is not good. It is foolish! The world suggests consensus, what is everyone else doing, the world suggests situational ethics, the ends justify the means, the world suggests "common" sense (if it is common it is man's wisdom), the world suggests moral relativism which is a morality that is expedient rather than absolute. But God has the answers! Jesus is the WAY, TRUTH, AND LIFE! The Spirit guides us into holiness! The Scriptures lead us to God's way! **Psalm 119:105** *Your word is a lamp to my feet and a light for my path.*

Ask Jesus to expose your triggers (you already know most of them) that they may NOT catch you off guard. He knows ALL of them! **Hebrews 2:18** *Because he himself suffered when he was tempted, he is able to help those who are being tempted.* God is not unaware of what you are facing and is ready, willing and able to deliver you: **1 Corinthians 10:13** *No temptation has seized you except what is common to man. And God is faithful; he will not let you be tempted beyond what you can bear. But when you are tempted, he will also provide a way out so that you can stand up under it.* In this passage we see that you are NOT unique! Rather, you are what is common to man. Your habits, addictions are not something new or rare, they do not surprise God. He has seen them and has wisdom to help you LIVE FREE! Ask him for it. The end result will prove to be awesome and you will have a personal testimony to the power of God. **James 1:12** (NLT) *God blesses those who patiently endure testing and temptation. Afterward they will receive the crown of life that God has promised to those who love him.*[2] Disengage your triggers: LIVE FREE!

HONEST QUESTIONS LEADING TO FREEDOM

1. What are triggers?

2. What are your triggers?

3. When are you most vulnerable to temptation?

4. Have you fully disclosed your triggers and vulnerability to God and your posse?

5. Are you continually asking God for his delivering wisdom?

Notes and Thoughts:

CHAPTER 12
LOVING LIFE

Many people struggle with the idea of life without their unwanted habits and/or their addictions. What would life be like without ... (fill in your struggle here)? Some of you would leap for joy; you are sooooo ready to live free. Others of you are saying to yourselves, "I wouldn't know what to do with myself if I didn't have ... (fill in your struggle here)." For instance, smokers often say they do not know what to do with their hands when they quit smoking. If you are used to watching pornography (and its related activities) you may not know how to use the free time you now have after Living free. These difficulties that attend the early days of Living free can be very serious and even drive a person back to the unwanted behavior. The key here is to begin to **LOVE LIVING FREE**!

One way to do this is to remember the bondage, the slavery you were under beforehand, but remember it without shame or guilt! You have been forgiven and totally set free! My mentor, Ralph Weaver, said to me one day when I was having a particularly difficult time understanding something he was trying to teach me (I think I had driven him to frustration), "Boy, you can learn; or you can get taught!" What an amazing lesson! The reason for him saying that has long disappeared from my memory but the concept is brilliant! Think of it this way. God is going to make me holy **1 Thessalonians 4:3a** *It is God's will that you should be sanctified:* (sanctified = made holy). Guess what, when God takes me into heaven, I WILL BE HOLY! Well then, what is left? I can **learn** to live holy, or I can be **TAUGHT** to live holy. If this needs further explanation, let me help you. God has outlined, in the Scriptures clearly, how he wants us to live, he has given us his Holy Spirit as a guide and reminder of his words, we can then **learn** (without consequences or discipline) to Live free; or we can **get taught** (experiencing consequences and discipline) how to Live free! Either way, the end result is the same. Some of us will come to this end with little or no scars; most of us will have a few; some of us will have very little unscarred flesh at the end.

> **1 Corinthians 3:10-15** *By the grace God has given me, I laid a foundation as an expert builder, and someone else is building on it. But each one should be careful how he builds. [11] For no one can lay any foundation other than the one already laid, which is Jesus Christ. [12] If any man builds on this foundation using gold, silver, costly stones, wood, hay or straw, [13] his work will be shown for what it is, because the Day will bring it to light. It will be revealed with fire, and the fire will test the quality of each man's work. [14] If what he has built survives, he will receive his reward. [15] If it is burned up, he will suffer loss; he himself will be saved, but only as one escaping through the flames.*

The grace of God gives us a foundation, holy and perfect to build our lives upon, that foundation is Jesus Christ and his perfect sacrifice for us, cleaning us up and setting us free. Then we begin to build! Our building materials are gold, silver, costly stones (these survive fire), wood, hay or straw (these perish in fire). [It should be clear to the reader that wood, hay and straw are the unwanted habits, idols, addictions, and sinful activities of our lives.] The key words are found at the end of verse 10, BUT EACH ONE SHOULD BE CAREFUL HOW HE BUILDS. Our lives are finite, God has purpose for our lives, that which he has prepared for us to accomplish. Let me re-quote **Ephesians 2:10** *For we are God's workmanship, created in Christ Jesus to do good works, which God prepared in advance for us to do.* When we do these things we build with gold, silver, and costly stones. The purpose of our lives, that which fills our bottomless pits perfectly, that which satisfies our souls, is to do the things for which God has made us and to LOVE THE LIFE HE HAS GIVEN US! When we waste our lives trying to fill up the abyss of our souls (bottomless pits of relationship and purpose) with things that will never satisfy (our habits and addictions) we build with wood, hay and straw. When the day of testing fire comes those who have built with gold, silver, costly gems will be rewarded, and the testing fire will consume the part of our lives that we built with wood, hay and straw. The end for the believer in Jesus is the same: Eternal Life! Either we enter with reward or as one escaping through the flames the choice is ours. Now it is not as clear-cut as all that. It is **never** too late to begin to Live free! It is **never** too late to begin to allow God to fill us to overflowing with relationship and purpose. But my desperate plea is that you BEGIN NOW! Do not waste another minute on that which is nothing, that which cannot satisfy. Be free, love the life God has planned for you, stay free once you are free and build with gold, silver and costly stones; live life with God and those whom he has given you (relationship); accomplish those things he has prepared you to do, serve him with all your heart (purpose)! Relish this Life of freedom; worship him who gives it to you. JUST IN CASE YOU DO NOT "LEARN" THIS, GOD HAS HIS WAYS OF "TEACHING YOU."

> **Hebrews 12:10-11** *Our fathers disciplined us for a little while as they thought best; but God disciplines us for our good, that we may share in his holiness.* ¹¹ *No discipline seems pleasant at the time, but painful. Later on, however, it produces a harvest of righteousness and peace for those who have been trained by it.*

Here we see a comparison to earthly fathers raising children, disciplining them to grow up well, as best as they can. God's discipline is good and his purpose is for us to share in his holiness! "Getting taught" is painful! [Remember we could learn (painless), or get taught (painful)]. The result of learning or getting taught is a harvest of righteous and peace, when we finally have it! Most of us learn some and get taught some. After forty years of walking with Jesus in faith and getting taught plenty; I wholeheartedly recommend LEARNING!

Learning to LOVE our new life is the process of taking off and putting on.

> **Colossians 3:9-10** *Do not lie to each other, since you have taken off your old self with its practices [10] and have put on the new self, which is being renewed in knowledge in the image of its Creator.*

You are made new, having left behind your old sinful life and the things you did before! Those things included your strategies (habits and addictions) to fill up your bottomless pits of relationship and purpose. Now in your new Life, your Life free of those old things you trust God to fill you up and make you like himself! Notice **verse 9** *Do not lie to each other*; this is an admonition to full disclosure. No secrets, no hidden motives; allow nothing to keep you in shame and guilt! The chains in the title of this book are not the behaviors themselves; these are merely the links in the chain. These behaviors are the result of the two bottomless pits that are like a black hole, a vacuum that demands to be filled. Behaviors (links) such as alcohol, drugs, gambling, pornography, sex, consumption (material possessions, eating, movies, internet, etc.), worry, and many more are symptoms of the emptiness of our souls demanding to be filled. *Broken Chains: freedom from unwanted habits and addictions* is about God filling our bottomless pits. When the relational pit is filled by God the chain that holds you in your emptiness disintegrates! The same with the bottomless pit for purpose, significance!

We must love living free! We must love the God who fills us with himself, his relationship, his purpose. **Psalm 90:14** *Satisfy us in the morning with your unfailing love, that we may sing for joy and be glad all our days.*

LOVE LIVING FREE!

This is your best defense against reverting to old strategies. **John 8:34-36** *Jesus replied, "I tell you the truth, everyone who sins is a slave to sin. [35] Now a slave has no permanent place in the family, but a son belongs to it forever. [36] So if the Son sets you free, you will be free indeed.* Slaves serve the family, but are not family members; they do not share the JOY of family membership. But a son belongs to the family forever! Jesus, the firstborn son sets you free from sin slavery, just ask him and trust him to do it. Ask him with every atom of your being, and then let him fill you to overflowing with relationship with him and the purpose, which he has for you in his kingdom. **Galatians 4:5-7** *God sent him to buy freedom for us who were slaves to the law, so that he could adopt us as his very own children. [6] And because we are his children, God has sent the Spirit of his Son into our hearts, prompting us to call out, "Abba, Father." [7] Now you are no longer a slave but God's own child. And since you are his child, God has made you his heir.* Relationship with God and knowing his purpose for you have MEANING, they are not the meaningless things you have used to try to fill yourself. **Hebrews 2:11** *Both the one who makes men holy and those who are made holy are of the same family. So Jesus is not ashamed to call them brothers.* This verse is about Jesus, he it is who makes us holy and we are declared to be his family, brothers! *So if the Son sets you free, you will be free indeed.* How can we not HATE the life of slavery? HOW CAN WE NOT LOVE THIS LIFE OF FREEDOM?

HONEST QUESTIONS LEADING TO FREEDOM

1. Do you love your habit or addiction?

   a. If you answer "no, I hate it," why do you hate it?

   b. If you answer "yes, I love it," why do you love it?

   c. If you answer, "it is a love/hate thing," list what you love and what you hate.

2. Answer, "What would life be like without (fill in your habit and/or addiction)"?

3. Determine if you want life free from your habit and/or addiction. Yes or No

4. Ask God to help you to LOVE LIVING FREE!

Notes and Thoughts:

F. Michael Grubbs

CHAPTER 13
LIVING CONNECTED

We have this insatiable, unquenchable pit that craves relationship, in our soul. We have come to know that only the INFINITE can fill this bottomless pit. Not only is God the only one ABLE to fill this emptiness, but HE WANTS TO FILL IT! Relationships need communication, conversation, sharing, and dialogue. As believers we want this desperately. God wants to converse with us more (we have not shed blood and died to converse with God, he has done so for us!). Therefore, prayer becomes paramount! This may not be, however, the kind of prayer you have been taught. This next section will be exploring that kind of communicating prayer that can be yours to foster a REAL RELATIONSHIP with God.

Hebrews 4:16 *Let us then approach the throne of grace with confidence, so that we may receive mercy and find grace to help us in our time of need.* God sits on the throne of grace with Jesus at his right side. This verse indicates that we can approach this throne with confidence, boldly. The purpose of our approach is to receive mercy and find grace and thereby get help when we need it. As we have already heard we can obtain this through the Scriptures, through wisdom, and through hearing. **God desires to**

speak with us. If you scheduled an appointment with me as your counselor (you are paying me a fee!) and I was fifteen minutes late for the appointment, I rushed into the coffee shop where we were meeting, put my briefcase on the table and began to tell you all about the things that made me late and what is going on in my life and twenty minutes later (you haven't spoken one word yet) I looked at my watch and declared myself late for my next appointment; I get up and leave you (taking your check with me); How are you feeling at this point? I know how you are feeling. You are angry. (You are also looking for another counselor.) You see this is what we do to God all the time. We tell him what is wrong, what we think he ought to do, what we are expecting him to do, then we get up and go on with our day without taking any time to listen! How ridiculous is this? I have said often to my clients that this represents HALF-PRAYING. It is only half of a conversation; God never gets the chance to speak! Unless I am very mistaken HIS half of the conversation is the MOST IMPORTANT HALF!

> **Ecclesiastes 5:1-2** *Guard your steps when you go to the house of God. Go near to listen rather than to offer the sacrifice of fools, who do not know that they do wrong. Do not be quick with your mouth, do not be hasty in your heart to utter anything before God. God is in heaven and you are on earth, so let your words be few.*

These are the words of Solomon, a very wise man, perhaps the wisest of the Old Testament. He is encouraging us not to be wrong-headed fools, but to LISTEN to God! Yes, we can tell him, like a father, all about our lives, he wants his little children to tell him everything about our lives (though he is already completely aware). But he wants us to LISTEN to his wisdom, his comfort, his direction, his solution. WE DESPERATELY NEED THIS! We need to hear that he loves us, that we are his children that he cares and has a plan for us and work for us to do that will please him. God has prepared a special place that we can go to hear from him.

Ephesians 2:6 (NLT) *For he raised us from the dead along* *with Christ and seated us with him in the heavenly realms because we are united with Christ Jesus.* When we became believers in Jesus Christ we were raised from the dead with him. (Read **Ephesians 2:1-5**) God then seated us with him! What do you need to be seated? **A chair!** I picture this chair like a Hollywood director's chair. It has my name printed on the back; the seat is contoured to my butt. It is specially made and placed just for me (remember space and time are different in the heavenlies so there can be many chairs, billions, in the same spot yet God deals with each individually). When I sit in my chair, before the throne of Grace, in the heavenly realms, God will speak to me what he wants me to know, what I need. How often can I come to my chair? **John 10:9** *I am the gate; whoever enters through me will be saved. He will come in and go out, and find pasture.* Going in, to the chair, coming out, back into this world; the great thing is there are no limits. We can go as often as we want. Once you have enjoyed your chair you will want to spend much time there. What does God say? Anything he desires! What you need. Please do not go there with a heart that demands, insists, or, orders. Remember what Solomon said; don't do wrong with your mouth, don't be quick to speak, go to listen not to prove yourself a fool. You are dealing with GOD ALMIGHTY, GOD EVERYWHERE, GOD ALL-POWERFUL: who loves you and has ONLY the best in mind for you (no matter what you think is best).

Connecting with God is the most important thing you can do to Live free! You will come to know his love, care, and provision for you. You will begin to know his power, his knowledge, and his plan. What does he sound like? People report how they hear him differently. My own experience is that he sounds just like me when I talk with myself in my head: BUT I KNOW IT IS NOT ME. You will experience him exactly as you need to experience him.

The chair is the first place to go when you are tempted. **Hebrews 2:18** *Because he himself suffered when he was tempted, he is able to help those who are being tempted.* Jesus knows, he invites you to the throne in your time of need (when are we not in need?)(Reread: **Hebrews 4:16** above). Mercy and grace are to be found there. He bids you come, not to judge you but to give you help.

Connecting with other believers fills up the bottomless pit of your soul for relationship. It MUST be God first, then others lest we make an idol of another human being and regard marriage partners, family, friends as more important to fill us up than God. Remember only the infinite can fill up our emptiness, men are finite. We have tried this and it ends in utter failure!

God however, designed us to live in relationship with others. Jesus spoke of this concept when asked to sum up the commandments. **Matthew 22:37-39** *Jesus replied: "'Love the Lord your God with all your heart and with all your soul and with all your mind.' ³⁸ This is the first and greatest commandment. ³⁹ And the second is like it: 'Love your neighbor as yourself.'* We are commanded to love others. You cannot accomplish this from far away. This requires being intentional. Schedules, weariness, and daily tasks will conspire against you. You must be involved in other's lives to love them. You must be aware of their fear, their struggle, their anxiety and worry, their failure as well as their success, peace, joy, etc. in order to love them. We are to be in relationship with God and with others. When we find people we can trust, who love us, whom we can confide in and who will not run from our stuff but give us wisdom and aid; we have found what God designed for us in this life. Living life together with all the beauty and warts, all the joy and tears, all the music and noise, all the success and failure; then coming through to the end and finding ourselves whole and holy … this is what God has planned. Do not minimize the life of fellowship. John wrote to the church in general about fellowship and its importance. **1 John 1:3** *We proclaim to you what we have seen and heard, so that you also may have fellowship with us. And our fellowship is with the Father and with his Son, Jesus Christ. ⁴ We write this to make our joy complete.* Each of us proclaiming what we have seen and heard about God and life to each other, reminding each other of God's goodness and power, sharing our struggles and difficulties, hearing each other's testimonies of the overcoming power of God; this is fellowship! And our fellowship is with God! Relating with God and those he has given us to live life with. This provides complete joy.

HONEST QUESTIONS LEADING TO FREEDOM

1. What is prayer?

2. Will you take the challenge of sitting in your chair, listening?

3. Will you make the effort to connect with others specifically regarding Living Free?

4. How important is fellowship for you? Will you ask God to make it more important?

Notes and Thoughts:

CHAPTER 14
HONEST TESTIMONY

Jesus came to set us free! His desire is for you to be whole: spiritually, emotionally, and mentally. HE WILL NEVER GIVE UP ON YOU!

Honest testimony is the truth of your life. No embellishment, nothing left out. God has ordered your steps through your life and brought you to living free. THIS IS POWERFUL for the purpose he has called you. Your story is important. It is powerful to set others free! God works in you for his glory! Your story will give hope to those who are stuck in their impotent strategies to fill themselves! TELL IT AND TELL IT OFTEN. Tell it with brutal honesty. Tell it without shame. Within your story people who are trapped in habits and addictions will see that there is more to life and comprehend the possibility of freedom and fulfillment. As you tell it you also remind yourself of what God has done for you. Your story will bring great joy to you and those who hear it. Your story will cause people to praise God and desire to know him better. God is building in you a great testimony to his glory and power, now and forever.

ENDNOTES

Chapter 3

1   Merriam-Webster, I. (1996). Merriam-Webster's collegiate thesaurus. Springfield, Mass.: Merriam-Webster.

Chapter 4

1   Merriam-Webster, I. (2003). *Merriam-Webster's collegiate dictionary*. (Eleventh ed.). Springfield, Mass.: Merriam-Webster, Inc.

2   Dr. Randy Hyde   www. Candeocan.com 2/24/10

PART 2 LIBERATION

Chapter 7

1   Wuest, K. S. (1997). *Wuest's word studies from the Greek New Testament: For the English reader* (1 Jn 2:15). Grand Rapids: Eerdmans.

Chapter 9

1   Griffin, E. A., & Griffin, E. (1997). *Getting together: A guide for good groups*. Downers Grove, Ill.: InterVarsity Press.

ABOUT THE AUTHOR

Dr. F. Michael Grubbs is the Christian Counselor and Coach at The Lyndon Center in Kansas City. With over 35 years in pastoral ministry, he has encouraged many in their walk towards freedom and the abundant life Jesus Christ offers. He holds a MS in Christian Counseling from Cairn University; Langhorne, PA and a Doctor of Counseling from Midwestern Baptist Theological Seminary, Kansas City, MO.

ABOUT THE LYNDON CENTER

The purpose of The Lyndon Center is to offer Christian counseling and coaching which integrates biblical truths. The goal is to aid each person served to achieve healthy emotional and spiritual potential within the context of Christian principles. More information is available at www.thelyndoncenter.com.